JUST THE JOB!

I work in a Garden Centre

by Clare Oliver

Photography by Chris Fairclough

FRANKLIN WATTS
LONDON • SYDNEY

© 2001 Franklin Watts

First published in 2001 by
Franklin Watts
96 Leonard Street
London
EC2A 4XD

Franklin Watts Australia
56 O'Riordan Street
Alexandria
NSW 2015

ISBN: 0 7496 4054 5
Dewey Decimal Classification 635
A CIP catalogue reference for this book is available
from the British Library

Printed in Malaysia

Editor: Kate Banham
Consultant: Beverley Mathias, REACH
Designer: Joelle Wheelwright
Art Direction: Jason Anscomb
Photography: Chris Fairclough

Acknowledgements
The publishers would like to thank Derek Edwards,
Shaw Trust and the staff at Percy Thrower's Garden
Centre, Shrewsbury, for their help in the production
of this book.

Shaw Trust is a leading national charity enabling disabled and
disadvantaged people to find routes to work. Each year, Shaw Trust
supports over 10,000 people through job preparation, job finding,
job support, job creation and job retention. For further information,
call 01225 716350, minicom 0345 697288, or log on to:
www.shaw-trust.org.uk

Contents

Meet Derek	6
The Garden Centre	8
First Tasks	10
Doing the Rounds	12
Delivery Time!	14
Taking a Break	16
The Aquatic Centre	18
The Potting Shed	20
Afternoon Tasks	22
Pros ... and Cons	24
Finding a Job	26
Glossary	28
Find Out More	29
Index	30

(Note: words printed in **bold italics** are explained in the glossary.)

Do you like being outside in the garden? Imagine if that was where you worked! Derek loves the outdoor life and has worked in his local garden centre for the last 11 years. Before that, he worked on a farm.

Derek's working day begins at 8 a.m. and finishes at 6 p.m. He is responsible for clearing rubbish and collecting the post. Certain areas of the garden centre are under his care, so he must keep them neat and tidy.

Derek drives to the garden centre on his scooter.

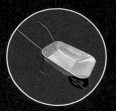

Favourite Five

Derek loves working with plants. His favourite types are flowers:

1. Pansy
2. Lavender
3. Geranium
4. Nasturtium
5. Rose

Derek likes pansies because they come in such bright, cheerful colours.

JUST THE JOB!

Garden Centre Assistant

Derek's most important *duties* are:

- Watering the plants
- Keeping his areas tidy
- Clearing rubbish
- Collecting and posting the mail
- Unloading deliveries

D erek works hard all day, but he gets an hour off for lunch and there are two short breaks in the morning and afternoon, too.

The garden centre was set up by Percy Thrower, a famous gardener who used to appear on television.

The Garden Centre

he garden centre where Derek works is a family business. It is run by three sisters.

Outdoors, there are lots of plants for sale, as well as garden ornaments, pots and huge bags of compost and bark.

Ann, Margaret and Sue run the garden centre. Their father, Percy Thrower, started the business in 1969.

The garden centre has a shop that sells house plants, seeds, bulbs and gardening tools. There is also a gift area, where books, candles and other items are sold.

In the garden centre is a coffee shop where cakes, sandwiches and hot meals are served. Many of the staff have their lunch there.

The coffee shop looks on to an open area, so customers can see the items for sale.

These areas are all run by the garden centre, but there are also a few other businesses on the site that pay rent to the garden centre. These are called **concessions**, and include a swimming pool shop, an **aquatic centre** and a **delicatessen**.

In the delicatessen, John arranges the jars of jams and pickles in an eye-catching display.

Managing a Shop

John manages the delicatessen. His duties include:

- Serving customers and offering them advice
- Cleaning the refrigerators and sweeping the shop
- Cashing up at the end of the day
- Ordering and checking deliveries
- Arranging tasting sessions

First Tasks

When Derek arrives at work at 8 a.m., he reports to his *supervisor*, Mark. Mark tells Derek what jobs need doing.

Mark talks with Derek each morning, and tells him his duties for the day.

Derek's first job each morning is to water the plants. Derek has about an hour before customers start arriving. It's best to use the hose when there is no one around who might get sprayed by accident! Even so, in very hot weather, Derek has to do extra watering in the afternoon.

Supervisor

Mark is in charge of other garden centre staff as well as Derek. Mark's jobs include:

- Sharing the jobs between his staff
- Checking that the jobs are done properly
- Ordering new *stock*, and checking deliveries
- Agreeing his staff's holidays – so they don't all take time off at once!
- Organising training for his staff

Each member of staff is responsible for particular areas of the garden centre. Derek looks after the display area of stone troughs in front of the coffee bar, and also part of the plant display area. He rakes the gravel and removes any rubbish that might have fallen into the troughs and pots.

Derek rakes the area in front of the coffee shop, to clear up any fallen leaves or litter.

On a hot, dry day, Derek might water these thirsty chrysanthemums three or four times.

Top Tips

Derek hoses the plants gently so their leaves and flowers are not battered. He gives them a good soaking, because small pots can soon dry out. At the same time, he looks for any sign of pests, such as *aphids* on the stems or slimy slugs on the bottom of the pots.

Doing the Rounds

After watering and tidying up, Derek gets rid of any rubbish that he has raked up. Then he tours the site collecting everyone else's rubbish, too. He empties all the bins and visits the different buildings at the garden centre, including the offices, coffee shop kitchens, customer toilets and all the shops. This gives Derek an opportunity to say good morning to the other staff.

Derek empties waste from the office bin into an old, empty compost bag.

As he goes, Derek sorts the rubbish so it will be easier to dispose of later. Old leaves and dead plants go on the compost heap. About once a month, a local farmer collects the compost, and uses it to *fertilise* his fields.

O ld cardboard boxes or paper waste from the shops and office are burned. Any other waste, such as drinks cans or plastics, are tossed into a **skip**. The skip hire company take away the skip when it is full and drop off a new, empty one.

Derek burns all the old boxes that come from the shop, from products such as plant feed and bulbs.

A customer trolley is ideal for collecting litter from the grounds.

Top Tips

The burner is far away from the parts of the garden centre where customers go. Even so, Derek checks the direction of the wind before he puts in more rubbish, and only does this when flames from any previous rubbish have died down.

Delivery Time!

Most deliveries happen on Fridays and Mondays. This is so that the centre can be sure of being well-stocked for the weekend rush, and then top up its supplies after the weekend. However, there are also other deliveries through the week, of everything from compost to cuttings.

Rob, the van driver, helps with the unloading. He puts any delicate items on to a trolley.

BRIERLEY
PLANTS
381769

Derek pulls the steel trolley of plants away from the van.

Huge lorries bring the bulkier items, such as sacks of compost, gravel and bark chippings. These are driven up to the storage barn and unloaded on wooden trays called **pallets**. Derek transports the laden pallets to the right area of the storage barn on his **forklift truck**.

Derek uses the forklift to shift empty pallets, too. ▼

Top Tips

Derek always wears steel-toed boots to work in case anything drops on his feet, but for driving the forklift he also puts on a hard hat. Derek had to have training and pass a special driving test to get his forklift truck licence. He must resit the test every three years, to check he hasn't got into any bad habits. A forklift can roll over if it isn't driven properly.

Smaller lorries and vans deliver plants, **cuttings** and stock for the shop. On quiet days, these can be unloaded in the customer car park. The goods come on steel trolleys that can be wheeled directly to the display areas.

Taking a Break

At about 10.30 a.m. Derek takes his first break of the day. All the staff gather in a corner of the shop and someone fetches hot and cold drinks and biscuits from the coffee shop. The staff also meet here for their mid-afternoon break.

The staff take their tea breaks in the shop.

Derek usually stops for lunch at 1 p.m. He buys a proper cooked lunch in the coffee shop and, like all the staff, he gets a discount.

Derek lives alone, and eating at the coffee shop means that he doesn't have to cook in the evening. Derek does a very physical job, so it's important that he has a proper meal each day.

Derek likes to visit Jaws, a 20-year-old koi carp that lives in the shop.

Kitchen Staff

Lunch is the busiest time, but the kitchen staff are busy all day:

- Baking fresh cakes
- Cooking hot meals
- Preparing sandwiches, snacks and other *refreshments*
- Cleaning the chillers, cooker, sink, floor and wall tiles
- Chalking up the menu
- Serving customers
- Clearing tables

Pamela puts all the cakes into a chilled display cabinet. Customers help themselves and pay at the till.

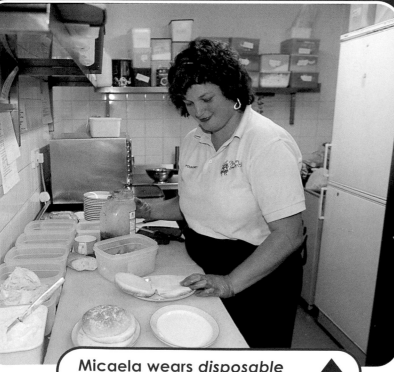

Micaela wears *disposable* gloves when handling food.

Favourite Five

All of the cakes in the coffee shop are home-made.
The best-sellers are:

1. Coffee and walnut cake
2. Carrot cake
3. Eccles cake
4. Chocolate cake
5. Lemon cake

The Aquatic Centre

Derek often spends part of his lunch break visiting the aquatic centre to see all the amazing fish. Two very large tanks house fish that are not for sale. In one of these there is a shoal of piranhas.

▲ The tinfoil barbs and silver dollars in this tank are just for display.

Favourite Five

Derek's favourite aquarium fish are:

1. Red-belly piranha
2. Neon tetra
3. Black moor
4. Zebra fish
5. Catfish

Glynn is the manager of the aquatic centre. He makes sure that all the tanks are clean and that the fish are healthy. He also advises customers on how to look after their fish – how to treat illnesses, which plants are best for an *aquarium*, and how to deal with *algae* and other problems. Most of the fish are tropical, but there are a few coldwater fish for ponds, too.

18

Aquatic Centre Assistant

Workers in the aquatic centre have to learn to recognise the different kinds of fish. Their other tasks include:

- Feeding the fish
- Cleaning the tanks
- Serving customers
- Arranging displays of tanks and accessories

Mark is cleaning one of the tanks. He uses a tube to siphon off any debris from the bottom into a bucket.

Derek pops into the aquatic centre during his lunch break to see Glynn and Tracey who work there.

The Potting Shed

As well as being responsible for his own areas, Derek helps out elsewhere when times are busy. He often goes to help Georgina in the potting greenhouse. At this garden centre, many of the plants are bought in as tiny **plug plants**, cuttings and seedlings. Georgina pots these on and **cultivates** them until they are big enough to put on sale.

Derek takes away the trays that Georgina has finished.

The garden centre is famous for its fuchsias. Georgina shows Derek how to root fuchsia cuttings.

At different times of the year, different plants are being grown, ready for the following season.

In spring, summer bedding plants such as geraniums are cultivated. In summer, Georgina takes cuttings from existing plants. She dips them in rooting powder and plants them in trays.

In autumn, the main plants are autumn crocuses and cyclamen, plus indoor bulbs and poinsettia ready for Christmas. In winter, Georgina plants daffodils and tulips ready for spring.

Georgina shows Derek how to pluck yellowing leaves from the busy-lizzies. ▶

Essential Kit

When Georgina needs Derek's help she calls him on his walkie-talkie. Derek's other essential kit includes:

- Sweatshirt and jeans
- T-shirt
- Waterproof jacket
- Strong boots
- Gardening gloves to protect his hands

The jacket, sweatshirt and T-shirt all feature the garden centre's logo, so customers can easily identify the staff.

Like all the garden centre staff, ▼ Derek carries a walkie-talkie.

Afternoon Tasks

Throughout the afternoon, Derek tidies the areas that he is responsible for. He removes any weeds from the paths and pots of plants. He also checks that the plant labels look shiny and new, and replaces them if they have faded.

Derek checks that each plant has a label with its name, growing requirements and price.

Derek weeds along the paths in his areas.

After his tea break, Derek tours the site to see if anyone has any mail that needs posting. Having one person responsible for doing this is efficient and saves time and money. Maureen, the office administrator, usually has the most mail.

Administrator

Maureen is the garden centre's administrator. She writes letters for the directors, and organises events such as flower-arranging classes. She also sorts out the printing and sending out of *mail shots*. These are colourful catalogues that tell customers about special offers and tempt them to visit by suggesting clever planting ideas.

JUST THE JOB!

Derek collects Maureen's mail just before 4 p.m. every afternoon. ▼

Derek takes all the letters to the post box just outside the garden centre gates. ▼

Pros ... and Cons

Derek loves being outdoors, so working at a garden centre is ideal. It's lovely to work among sweet-smelling flowers and beautiful plants. Even so, being outdoors is not so much fun when it's raining or bitterly cold. It's tiring being on your feet all day, too, and there is lots of heavy carrying to do.

Working outside is fine in the summer, but not so enjoyable as winter sets in.

Customers often ask Derek to lift heavy items on to their trolley.

Being in charge of particular areas gives Derek a sense of pride. He can see the results of his efforts when he looks at the neat rows of plants.

Driving the forklift is Derek's favourite job. Getting his licence really boosted his confidence. The test is difficult, and not everyone manages to pass.

erek is one of the longest-serving employees at the garden centre. Despite the hard work it is a very relaxed place. Derek is very happy there.

Derek often has to throw rubbish into the skip. This involves a lot of bending and lifting, which can be very tiring.

All the staff at the garden centre get a discount at the shops on the site. Derek buys his favourite cheese at the delicatessen.

Finding a Job

The only *qualifications* for working at a garden centre are that, like Derek, you are strong, fit and healthy. You also need to love being outside, and it helps if you are interested in plants.

You have to enjoy dealing with customers – showing them the way, helping them with their shopping, or even working on the cash desk. You also have to get on well with the other workers, so it's not a job for someone who prefers being on their own.

Derek is always ready to help customers if they need it.

At the end of the day, Derek collects all the trolleys, ready for tomorrow.

Job Know-How

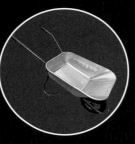

What qualifications do I need?

None. You need a special licence to drive a forklift truck, but training for this would happen on the job.

What personal qualities do I need?

Responsible and reliable. Healthy, energetic and strong. Some knowledge of plants and gardening.

How do I apply?

Watch the local press for adverts, or contact your nearest garden centre direct and ask if they need extra help. Derek had special needs, so a charity, the Shaw Trust, helped to find him work.

Will there be an interview?

Yes – to check how well you get on with people, as you will have contact with customers.

Tracey is on work experience at the aquatic centre. She uses a small net to bag up a fish for a customer.

Many schools organise *work experience*, and you could ask to be placed at a garden centre. You could also try to get a Saturday job there while you are still at school. You may even find that, when you leave school, the garden centre can offer you full-time work.

Margaret works for the Shaw Trust who helped Derek find his job. She visits him at work about every four months.

Glossary

Algae	Water plants that can choke a pond.
Aphids	Bugs that feed on plant juices and carry plant diseases.
Aquarium	A tank for keeping fish.
Aquatic centre	A shop that sells pet fish.
Concession	A business that is allowed to be on the property of a larger business.
Cultivate	To look after something and make it grow.
Cutting	A small stem from a growing plant that is cut off and made to grow into a new plant.
Delicatessen	A shop that sells cheese, eggs, cooked meats and preserves.
Disposable	Throw-away.
Duties	Jobs that must be done.
Fertilise	Add goodness and nutrients to crops and soil.
Forklift truck	A truck with steel prongs in front that can transport heavy goods, especially on pallets.
Mail shot	Advertisements or catalogues that are sent to lots of people.
Pallet	A wooden tray for stacking goods. Its double base allows a forklift truck to lift it.
Plug plant	A tiny plant that is ready to go in a bigger pot.
Qualifications	Official requirements for a particular job.
Refreshments	Drinks and snacks.
Skip	A metal container used as a giant bin for rubbish.
Stock	Goods for sale in a shop.
Supervisor	Someone who supervises (watches over) someone's work.
Work experience	An unpaid period of work, often for a week, so that a person can see what a job is like at first-hand.

Find Out More

Visit the garden centre where Derek works:

Percy Thrower's Garden Centre
Oteley Road
Shrewsbury
SHROPS SY2 6QW

Visit this website to find out the names and addresses of garden centres in your area:
www.gardening.centre-uk.com

Visit this website to find out loads about gardening:
www.bbc.co.uk/gardening

There are lots of magazines specially for people interested in gardening. Look in your local newsagent for:
BBC Gardeners World
Gardens Illustrated

Join this society to learn more about plants and gardens, or to find out about local gardening clubs:
Royal Horticultural Society (RHS)
80 Vincent Square
London SW1P 2PE

In Australia you can contact:
Australian Institute of Horticulture
15 Bowen Crescent
West Gosford, NSW 2250

Nursery Institute of Australia
Suite 402/16–18 Cambridge Street
Epping, NSW 2121

Australian Nurseries Online
www.nurseriesonline.com.au
Email: info@nurseriesonline.com.au

Also, why don't you...
• Visit your local library and check out the careers section.
• Look in your local library for books about gardens and plants, too.
• Find out if there is a teacher at your school who is an expert careers advisor.
• Look in your local business directory under 'Garden Centres' to find out who to contact for work experience placements.

Index

administrator 23
application 27
aquatic centre 9, 18–19, 27, 28

burner 13

clothing 15, 21
coffee shop 8, 11, 12, 16–17
compost heap 12
concessions 9, 12, 18–19,
    25, 28
customers 10, 13, 17, 19, 23,
    24, 26, 27
cuttings 14–15, 20, 28

delicatessen 9, 25, 28
deliveries 7, 9, 10, 14, 15
display areas 9, 11, 17, 19
driving test 15, 24

fish 16, 18–19, 28
forklift truck 15, 24, 27, 28

holidays 10

interview 27

kitchen staff 17

money 9, 26

outdoor life 6, 24, 26

pests 11, 28
plants 7, 8, 10, 11, 14, 15,
    20–21, 22, 24, 27, 28
post 6, 7, 23
potting shed 20-21

qualifications 26–27, 28

raking 11
responsibility 6, 11, 20, 22, 23,
    24, 27
rubbish 6, 7, 11, 12–13, 25, 28

safety 13, 15
Saturday job 27
shop manager 9
storage barn 15
supervisor 10, 28

Thrower, Percy 7, 8, 29
tidying 6, 7, 11, 12–13, 22
training 10, 15, 27

walkie-talkie 21
watering 7, 10, 11, 12
weeding 22
work experience 27, 28, 29
working hours 6, 7, 16